THE SHADOW WORK JOURNAL

FOR COUPLES

CALLIE PARKER

Download the Audiobook Version for
FREE

If you love listening to audiobooks on-the-go, you can download the audiobook version of this book for FREE just by signing up for a FREE 30-day audible trial!

Scan the QR code or click the links below to get started

>> For Audible US <<

>> For Audible UK <<

>> For Audible FR <<

>> For Audible DE <<

>>For Audible CA<<

>>For Audible AU<<

WELCOME TO
UNLOCKING HAPPINESS

YOUR GUIDE TO ACTIVITIES THAT BOOST YOUR MOOD

Embark on a journey to elevate your daily mood and harness the transformative power of happiness. Inside these pages, you'll discover the scientific underpinnings of how activities can significantly boost your well-being and learn why embracing new experiences is key to a fulfilling life.

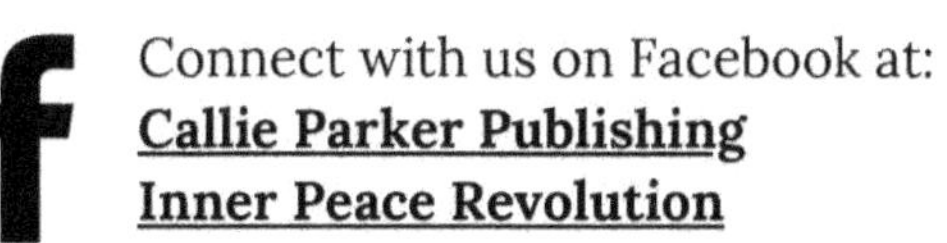

What Will You Gain from This eBook?

- Science-Backed Insights
- Practical Strategies
- Daily Habits
- Inspiring Activties
- Creative and Social Pursuits
- Mindfulness and Relaxation Techniques
- Customizable Planner

Ready to Boost Your Happiness? Start your journey now! Scan the QR code or follow the link below to join our newsletter for exclusive content, and begin building your joyful life today.

Send me my free e-book <u>Unlocking Happiness</u>

Connect with us on Facebook at:
Callie Parker Publishing
Inner Peace Revolution

ELEVATE YOUR JOURNEY WITH THE *SHADOW WORK FOR COUPLES* BOOK

While this journal is a valuable tool for reflection and exploration, it's designed to be most effective when used alongside its companion book, Shadow Work for Couples. To truly unlock the transformative potential of this process, consider diving into the comprehensive guidance and insights offered in the book. Here's how it will elevate your experience:

- Build a Strong Foundation: The book lays the groundwork for understanding the complex concepts of shadow work, providing the theoretical and practical knowledge needed to navigate this journey effectively.
- Gain Deeper Insights: Shadow Work for Couples delves into the nuances of individual and shared shadows, offering a broader perspective on the challenges and opportunities for growth within your relationship.
- Tailored Guidance for Every Stage: The book provides step-by-step instructions and support, guiding you through each phase of the shadow work process, ensuring you and your partner feel equipped and empowered every step of the way.
- Personalized Action Plans: Shadow Work for Couples offers tools and techniques for creating personalized action plans based on your specific needs and goals as a couple, helping you translate insights into real-world change.
- Create Lasting Transformation: By combining the book's comprehensive knowledge with the journal's personalized reflection space, you'll create a powerful synergy that leads to lasting positive change in your relationship.

Embrace the full potential of your shadow work journey by pairing this journal with the Shadow Work for Couples book. It's the key to unlocking a deeper understanding of yourselves, your partner, and the incredible love story you're creating together.

Introduction to The Shadow Work Journal for Couples

Welcome to *The Shadow Work Journal for Couples*. This journal is designed to be your companion as you explore the transformative practices presented in Shadow Work for Couples. Together, you and your partner will embark on a journey of self-discovery, vulnerability, and profound connection.

In *Shadow Work for Couples*, we look into the often-hidden aspects of ourselves—our individual "shadows"—and explore how they impact our relationship dynamics. This journal provides a structured space for you and your partner to work through the exercises and reflections in each chapter, fostering greater understanding and intimacy.

Each section of this journal corresponds to a chapter in the book, offering prompts and activities designed to help you apply the concepts to your relationship. Through honest communication, shared reflection, and mutual support, you will uncover deeper layers of yourselves and your partnership, building a stronger, more resilient bond.

As you work through this journal together, approach each exercise with openness and curiosity. Allow yourselves to be vulnerable, sharing your thoughts and feelings honestly. This journal is a sacred space for you and your partner to explore, heal, and grow together.

Remember, this journey is unique to your relationship. Use this journal not only as a companion to the book but also as a testament to your commitment to nurturing a deeper, more authentic connection. Together, the book and journal will support you in navigating the complexities of intimacy, fostering mutual understanding, and cultivating a love that is truly transformative.

Purpose of the Journal

Within these pages, you and your partner will find more than just blank spaces. This journal is designed to serve multiple purposes on your shared journey of growth and connection:

- Mirror to Your Shared Soul: Often, the act of writing together can reveal hidden depths of understanding and emotions within your relationship. By reflecting on the guided prompts, you'll look deeper into your shared experiences, creating a more profound connection with your partner and yourselves.
- Safe Haven for Vulnerability: This journal is a judgment-free zone for both of you. Its sole purpose is to provide a confidential environment where you can both be raw, honest, and vulnerable with each other. Here, every emotion is valid, every thought acknowledged, and every fear can be shared without judgment.
- Healing Balm for Your Relationship: As you navigate life's ups and downs as a couple, you'll encounter a range of emotions and memories. Writing together can be therapeutic, allowing you to process past wounds, celebrate shared joys, and envision a future filled with love and understanding.
- Guide for Mutual Growth: The prompts are crafted not just for reflection but also for nurturing your relationship. They will challenge you to confront challenges, celebrate strengths, and co-create a future aligned with your shared values and aspirations.
- A Testament to Your Love Story: Over time, this journal will become a tangible record of your growth as a couple. It will stand as a testament to your resilience, evolution, and the unique bond you share.

Remember, there's no right or wrong way to approach this journal. It's your story, your voices, and your shared truth. Let's embark on this journey of deepening intimacy and connection together. May you find clarity, strength, and an even deeper understanding of your love along the way.

Importance of Reflection in Nurturing Intimacy

Reflection, the practice of intentionally examining our experiences and emotions, plays a crucial role in cultivating deeper intimacy within a relationship. While introspection is valuable for any individual, for couples, it takes on a unique significance as it allows for:

- Understanding Self and Partner: Couples bring their individual histories, perspectives, and triggers into a relationship. Reflection helps each partner understand their own inner workings and how they interact with their partner's. It allows for greater self-awareness and empathy, fostering a deeper understanding of each other's needs and desires.
- Strengthening Emotional Connection: By reflecting on shared experiences, both positive and challenging, couples can strengthen their emotional bond. It allows for the processing of emotions together, promoting empathy, vulnerability, and ultimately, a greater sense of connection.
- Resolving Conflict and Healing Wounds: Every relationship encounters conflicts and disagreements. Reflection can help couples identify underlying causes of tension, understand each other's perspectives, and find constructive solutions. It also facilitates healing from past hurts, fostering forgiveness, and rebuilding trust.
- Nurturing Shared Values and Goals: By reflecting on their shared values, dreams, and aspirations, couples can align their visions for the future. This shared understanding creates a sense of purpose and unity, strengthening their commitment to each other.
- Enhancing Communication and Intimacy: Reflection encourages open and honest communication. As partners learn to express their thoughts and feelings more clearly, they create a safe space for deeper intimacy and vulnerability.
- Renewing Passion and Commitment: Through reflection, couples can rekindle the spark in their relationship. By revisiting cherished memories and acknowledging their love and appreciation for each other, they can reignite passion and recommit to their

shared journey.

In essence, reflection serves as a catalyst for growth and intimacy within a relationship. It empowers couples to build a strong foundation of understanding, communication, and mutual support, ultimately leading to a more fulfilling and enduring partnership.

How to Use this Journal

Welcome to a space crafted specifically for you and your partner, a space where your collective voices, feelings, and experiences within your relationship take center stage. This guided journal is designed to be more than just a collection of moments; it's a tool for understanding, healing, and celebrating the unique journey you share as a couple. Here's how to make the most of it:

- Establish a Shared Routine: While spontaneity has its place, setting aside dedicated time for journaling together can foster consistency and create a ritual for connection and reflection. Whether it's a daily check-in, a weekly heart-to-heart, or a monthly deep dive, choose a cadence that suits your relationship.
- Create a Comfortable and Safe Space: Find a quiet, cozy spot where you both feel at ease and able to open up. This physical space can create a sanctuary for vulnerability, honesty, and emotional intimacy.
- Be Honest with Each Other: This journal is a private space for the two of you. There's no need to filter, edit, or censor your thoughts or feelings. Embrace authenticity, allowing your true selves to shine through and deepening your connection.
- Engage with the Prompts: Throughout this journal, you'll find prompts designed to spark meaningful conversations and guide your reflections as a couple. Use them as starting points, but feel free to explore whatever topics arise naturally and resonate with your relationship.
- Revisit Past Entries Together: As you progress through this journal, take time to reread past entries together. This shared reflection can offer valuable insights into your growth as a couple, highlighting changes, challenges, and the beautiful moments that define your journey.
- Add Visuals or Personal Touches: Feel free to personalize your entries with sketches, doodles, photos, or anything else that captures the essence of your relationship. These visual elements can add depth and meaning to your shared reflections.
- Practice Mutual Compassion: Some reflections may bring up difficult emotions or memories. Be gentle with yourselves and each other. Offer support, understanding, and empathy as you

- navigate these shared experiences. If needed, seek guidance from a trusted therapist or counselor.
- Celebrate Your Love Story: Remember, every entry, whether filled with joy, sorrow, laughter, or tears, is a testament to the strength and resilience of your relationship. Celebrate each word, each emotion, and every milestone together.

This journal is your own unique love story in the making. There's no right or wrong way to use it. Embrace the journey, allow it to evolve alongside your relationship, and let this journal be a cherished companion on your path toward deeper understanding, acceptance, and unwavering love.

Guided Journal

TABLE OF CONTENTS

Introduction: How To Get Started

Chapter 1: Exploring Your Unconscious Mind
Individual reflections Individual exercises Indications and joint activities

Chapter 2: Accepting Repressed Desires
Individual reflections Individual exercises Indications and joint activities

Chapter 3: Understanding Projection
Individual reflections Individual exercises Indications and joint activities

Chapter 4: Integrating Your Shadow
Individual reflections Individual exercises Indications and joint activities

Chapter 5: Embarking on Your Journey of Individuation
Individual reflections Individual exercises Indications and joint activities

Chapter 6: Navigating Moral Ambiguity
Individual reflections Individual exercises Indications and joint activities

Chapter 7: Meeting Your True Self
Individual reflections Individual exercises Indications and joint activities

Chapter 8: Embrace Transformation
Individual reflections Individual exercises Indications and joint activities

Conclusion: Your Continued Journey in the Shadows

The Unconscious

The unconscious mind of man sees correctly even when the conscious reason is blind and powerless.

Carl Jung

Dream Insights

Reflect on a recent dream and write about the emotions and themes you observed. What could this dream reveal about your unconscious desires or fears?

Intuitive Choices

Think about a recent decision that you made more out of intuition than logic. Describe the decision and explore what unconscious factors might have influenced it.

Unexplained Emotional Reactions

Recall an incident when your emotional reaction surprised you.
Write about what unconscious memories or experiences might be
connected to this reaction.

Unexplained Emotional Reactions

Recall an incident when your emotional reaction surprised you.
Write about what unconscious memories or experiences might be
connected to this reaction.

Individual reflections

Meditation on the Unconscious
Spend 10 minutes in a quiet meditation, focusing on your breathing.
Allow your thoughts to flow freely and write down any ideas that
come to you about your unconscious mind.

Artistic Expression

Create a piece of art that represents a part of your inner self that you feel is hidden or unknown. Use colors, shapes and textures to express this invisible aspect.

Artistic Expression

Create a piece of art that represents a part of your inner self that you feel is hidden or unknown. Use colors, shapes and textures to express this invisible aspect.

Dialogue with the Unconscious

Write a letter to your unconscious mind. Ask questions about things you want to understand better about yourself. Then, write an answer from the perspective of your unconscious.

Dialogue with the Unconscious

Write a letter to your unconscious mind. Ask questions about things you want to understand better about yourself. Then, write an answer from the perspective of your unconscious.

Share a recent dream with your partner and discuss what it might mean about your unconscious thoughts and feelings. Encourage your partner to do the same and argue.

Each partner shares a story about a time when they acted on their intuition. Discuss what this might reveal about your unconscious mind.

Take turns acting out parts of your partner's unconscious personality that you have observed. Discuss the feelings and perceptions that arise from this exercise.

Joint Collage

Together, create a collage using images and words that you think represent your combined unconscious minds. Discuss the process and what each element could symbolize.

Unconscious
DESIRES AND FEARS

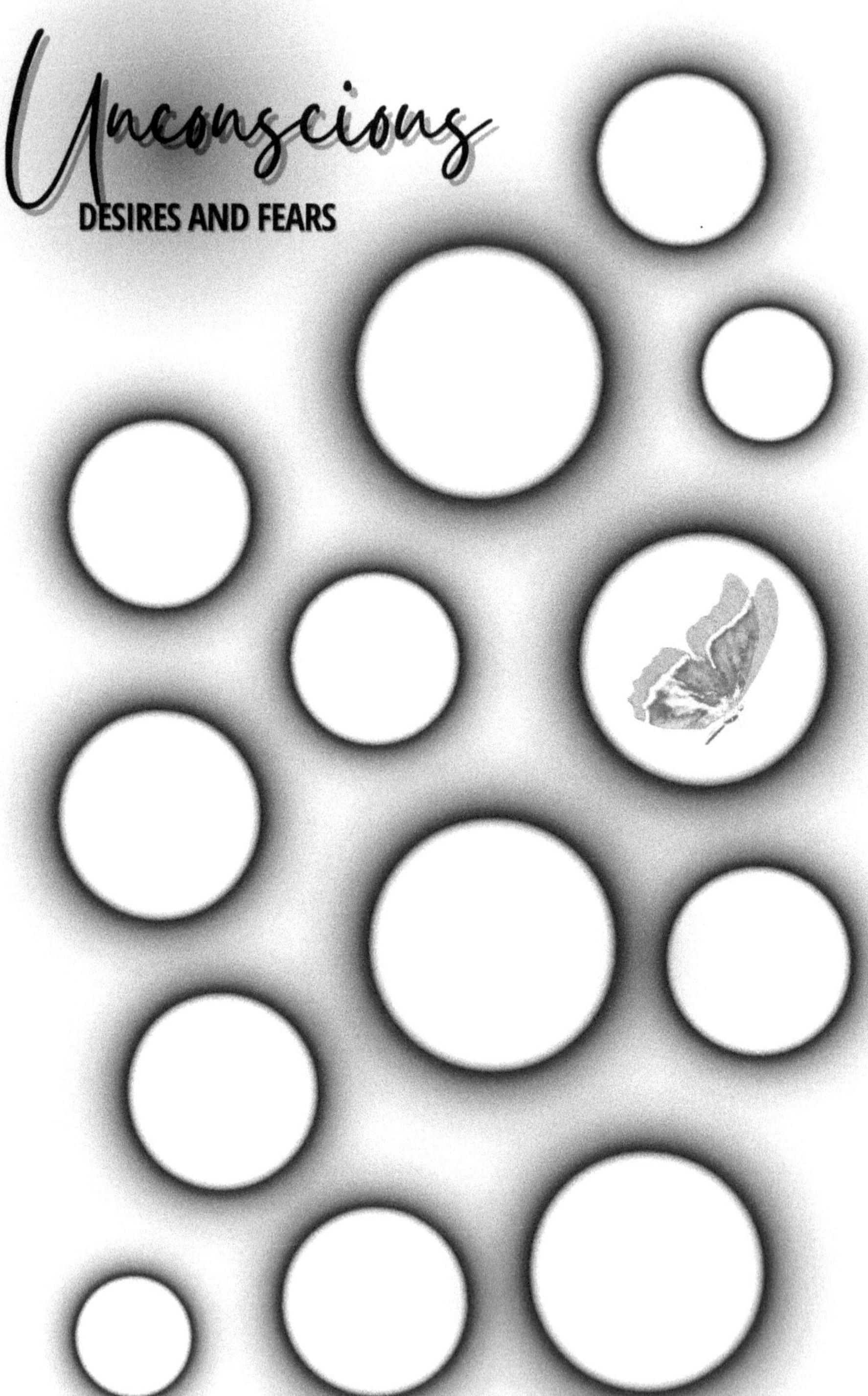

Take turns sharing a desire or fear that you think might arise from your unconscious mind. Discuss how these might influence your relationship and ways to support each other.

Repressed *desires*

The scariest thing is to accept yourself completely.

Carl Jung

Hidden Yearnings

Reflect on a desire that you have often left aside or hidden. Write about why you might be suppressing this desire and how it makes you feel.

Individual reflections

Conflicting Emotions

Consider a time when you felt conflicted about a decision. Explore any underlying desires you have been repressing that have contributed to this conflict.

Individual reflections

Forbidden Thoughts

Think of a thought or impulse that you have considered "forbidden" or unacceptable. Write about where this judgment might come from and how recognizing this thought makes you feel.

Desire Visualization

Find a quiet space to meditate.
Visualize yourself fulfilling a repressed
desire. Notice the emotions and
thoughts that arise during this
visualization.

Letter of Acknowledgment

Write a letter to yourself acknowledging a repressed desire. Details how accepting this wish could positively impact your life.

Create a 'desire map', a conceptual representation of repressed desires, their origins and how they might unconsciously manifest in someone's life. It includes several paths and nodes, each labeled with emotions or situations related to repressed desires, and shows both the origins and unconscious manifestations of these desires.

Create a 'desire map', a conceptual representation of repressed desires, their origins and how they might unconsciously manifest in someone's life. It includes several paths and nodes, each labeled with emotions or situations related to repressed desires, and shows both the origins and unconscious manifestations of these desires.

Take turns sharing a repressed desire with your partner. Discuss why you think you have repressed these desires and how you can support each other in recognizing them.

Talk to your partner about any emotional barriers that may prevent you from fulfilling your desires. Offer each other ideas and support.

It depicts a scenario in which each of you enacts a repressed desire in a safe and supportive environment. Discuss the feelings that arise from this exercise.

Creative Project

Engage together in a creative activity, such as painting or writing a story, that symbolizes your combined repressed desires. Reflect on the experience and what it reveals about each of you.

Together

Projection

Everything that irritates us about others can lead us to understand ourselves.

Carl Jung

Recognizing Projection

Reflect on a recent conflict or irritation with your partner. Write about what this might reveal about your own feelings or insecurities.

Individual reflections

Triggers in Projection

Identify a trait in your partner that consistently triggers a strong reaction in you. Explore how this trait might be something you're uncomfortable recognizing in yourself.

Unconscious Expectations

Consider an aspect of your relationship where you feel your partner is not meeting your expectations. Write about how these expectations might reflect your own unmet needs or desires.

Individual reflections

Journaling on Projection

For a week, keep a journal of times when you feel upset or upset with your partner. At the end of the week, review your entries to identify patterns that may indicate a projection.

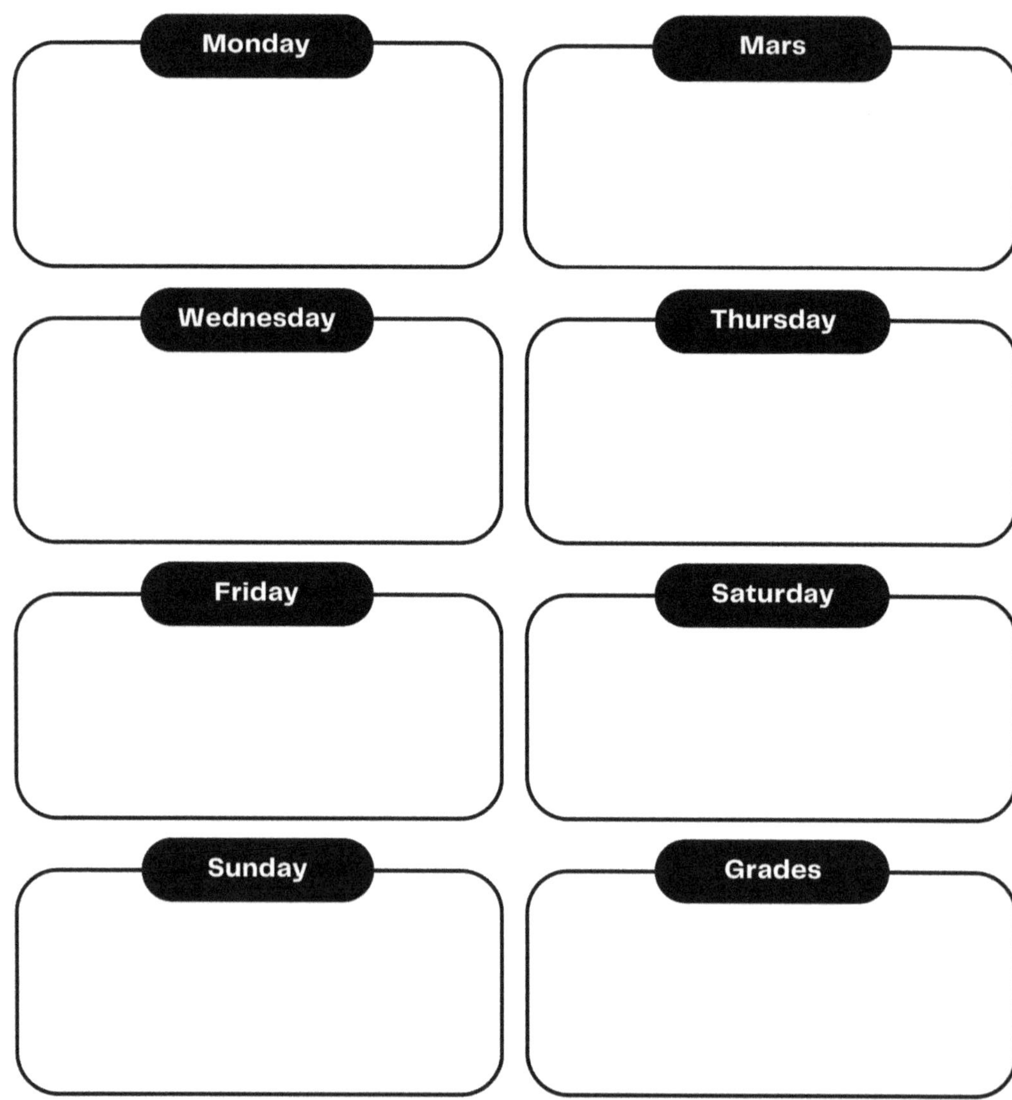

Journaling on Projection

For a week, keep a journal of times when you feel upset or upset with your partner. At the end of the week, review your entries to identify patterns that may indicate a projection.

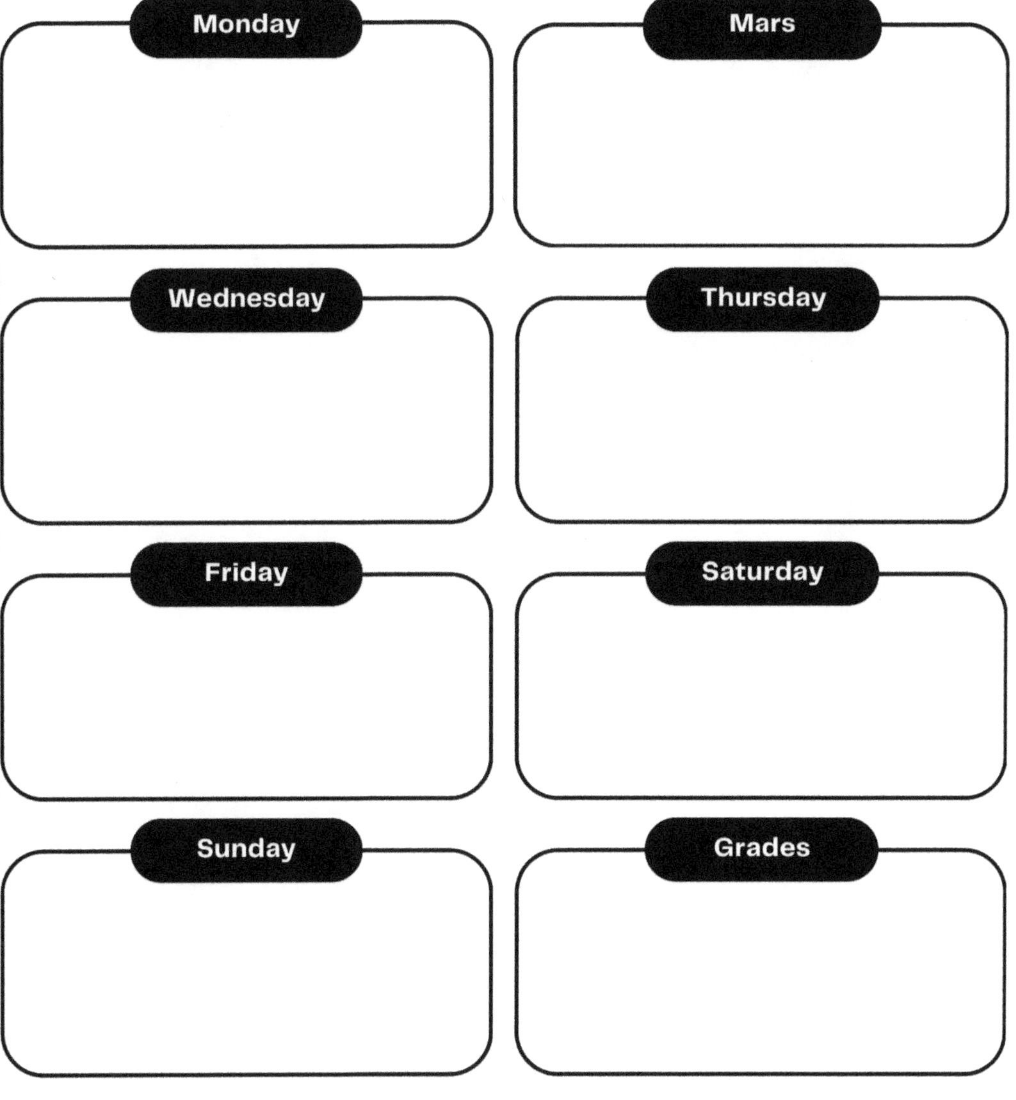

Meditation on Self-Acceptance

Practice a guided meditation focused on self-acceptance. Pay attention to any resistance that arises, as it may indicate areas of projection.

Share your ideas from the individual exercises with each other. Discuss ways you might project onto each other and how to address this.

Each partner shares a personal trigger and discusses its origins. Reflect on how understanding these triggers can reduce projection in your relationship.

Visualize a scenario in which you both transcend beyond your projections. Discuss what this scenario was like for each of you and how you felt.

Integration

One does not become enlightened by imagining figures of light, but by making the darkness conscious.

Carl Jung

Shadow Traits Acknowledgment

Identify a trait in yourself that you often avoid or dislike. Write about how recognizing and integrating this trait might benefit you.

Individual reflections

Moments of Integration

Remember a time when you successfully integrated a part of your shadow. Describe the situation and how it made you feel.

Individual reflections

Inner Resistance

Consider an aspect of your personality that you find difficult to accept. Write about the resistance you feel toward this aspect and why it might be there.

Shadow Dialogue

Spend some time writing a dialogue between you and your shadow aspect. What would this part of you say? How would you respond?

Artistic Representation

Create a work of art that represents your dark side integrating into your entire being. Use this as a form of acceptance and recognition.

Artistic Representation

Create a work of art that represents your dark side integrating into your entire being. Use this as a form of acceptance and recognition.

Together, identify the common shadow traits you both share. Discuss how these traits affect your relationship and ways to positively integrate them.

Take turns representing each other's dark aspects. This exercise can generate empathy and understanding of each other's internal struggles.

Discuss ways you can support each other in integrating your individual shadows, such as through affirmations, active listening, or shared activities.

Creating an Integration

Ritual Develop a small ritual or practice that symbolizes the integration of your shadows, to do together regularly.

Together

Individuation

The privilege of your life is to become who you really are.

Carl Jung

Personal Individuation Path

Reflect on your journey toward individuation. What are the key aspects of your personality or life experience that you believe are essential to your true self?

Individual reflections

Challenges to Individuation

Identify a challenge or obstacle you have faced on your journey of self-discovery. How did you get through it and what did you learn about yourself?

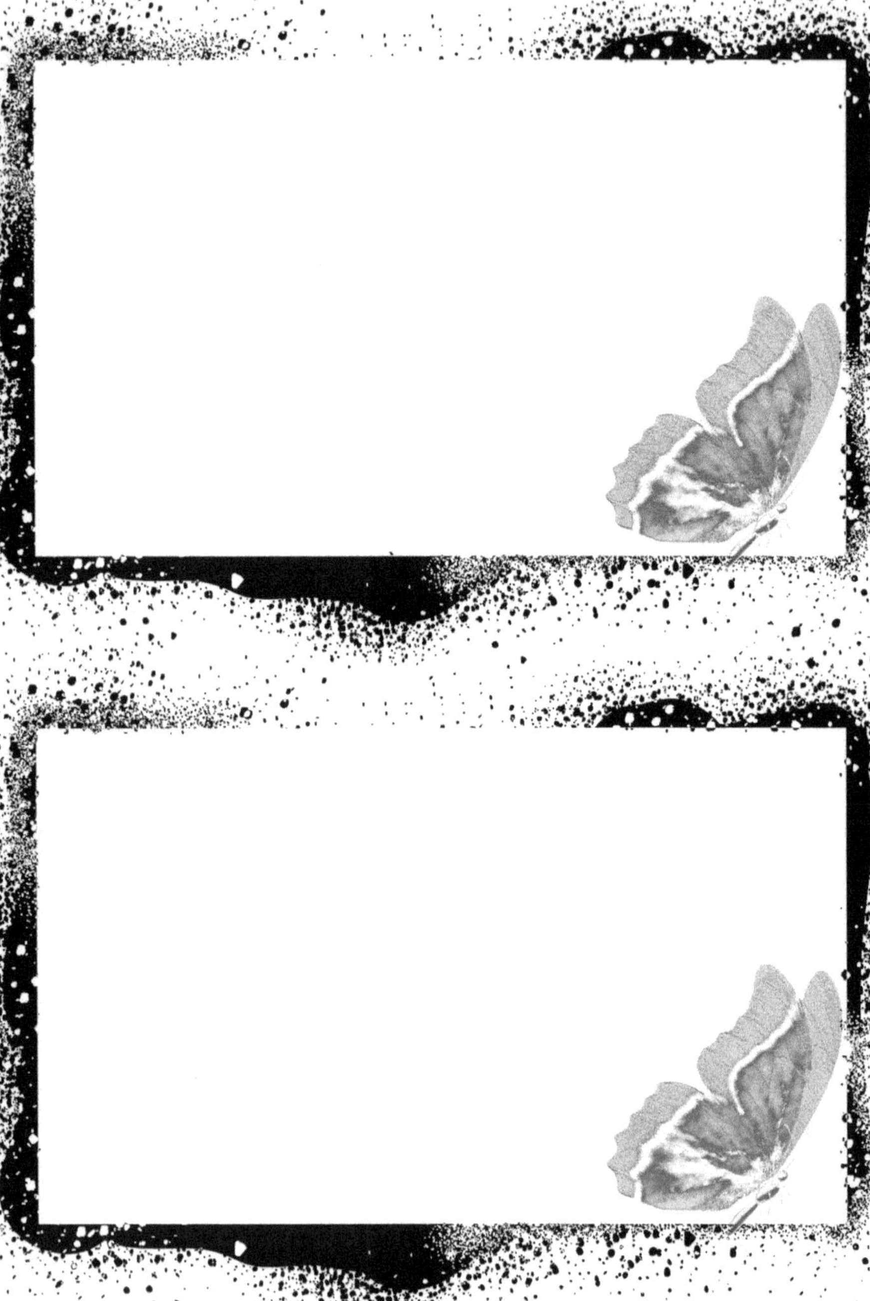

Future Self Visualization

Imagine your future self, having fully realized your potential. Write about what this looks like and how it is different from your current self.

Life Timeline

Create a timeline of your life, highlighting key moments that contributed to your individualization. Reflect on how each experience has shaped who you are.

Life Timeline

Create a timeline of your life, highlighting key moments that contributed to your individualization. Reflect on how each experience has shaped who you are.

Dialogue with the Future Self

Write a letter to your future self or have a mock conversation, discussing your hopes, fears, and questions about your journey of individuation.

Share your paths of personal individuation with each other. Discuss how these individual journeys complement and influence your relationship.

Identify and discuss the values that are important to both of you. How do these values support your individual and shared growth paths?

Take turns discussing a personal dream or aspiration. Offer feedback and support on how each partner can pursue their individual goals.

Together, create a vision board that represents your individual and shared aspirations. Use images and words to symbolize your hopes for the future.

For each of the categories below, write down the things you are doing well and the things you need to improve. Take time to reflect on these and write a goal for each category.

CATEGORY	WHAT I'M DOING RIGHT	WHERE DO I NEED TO IMPROVE?	MY GOALS
FAMILY			
FRIENDS			
WORK/SCHOOL			
BODY			
MENTAL HEALTH			
SPIRITUALITY			

Life GOALS

For each of the categories below, write down the things you are doing well and the things you need to improve. Take time to reflect on these and write a goal for each category.

CATEGORY	WHAT I'M DOING RIGHT	WHERE DO I NEED TO IMPROVE?	MY GOALS
FAMILY			
FRIENDS			
WORK/SCHOOL			
BODY			
MENTAL HEALTH			
SPIRITUALITY			

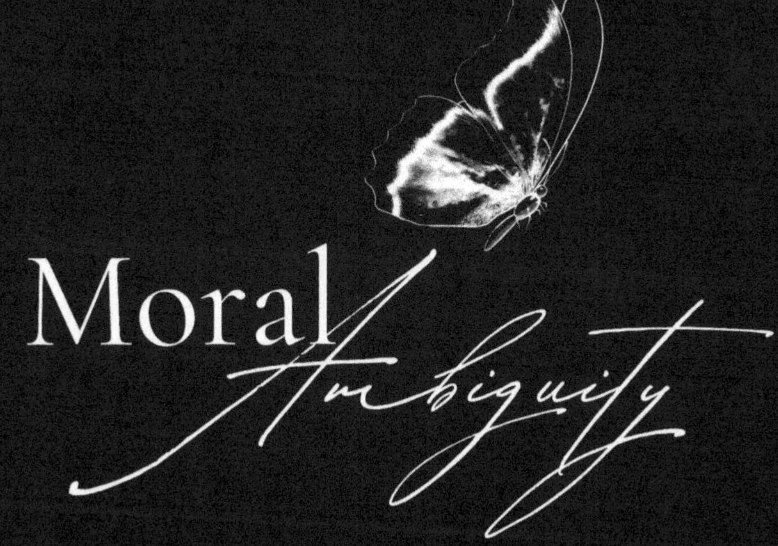

Moral *Ambiguity*

The ability to support oneself is very difficult, but it is the mark of a mature personality.

Carl Jung

Moral Dilemma Reflection

Think about a time when you were faced with a moral dilemma.
Write about the decisions you made and how you felt about them.
Was there any aspect of your decision that reflected moral
ambiguity?

Individual reflections

Personal Values Examination

Identify and write about your core values. Have there been times when these values were in conflict? How did you navigate these situations?

Understanding Complexity

Reflect on a situation in which you judged another person's actions.
In retrospect, can you see any moral ambiguity in that situation?
How does this change your perspective?

Individual reflections

1

2

3

4

5

Create a list of your top five values. For each value, write a
scenario in which this value could conflict with another.
Reflect on how you would resolve these conflicts.

1

2

3

4

5

Create a list of your top five values. For each value, write a scenario in which this value could conflict with another. Reflect on how you would resolve these conflicts.

Choose a historical or fictional event that involves a moral dilemma. Write an essay or short story from the perspective of a character facing this dilemma, exploring the complexities of their decision-making process.

Identify the shared values in your relationship. Discuss how these values have guided your decisions and actions as a couple, especially in complex situations.

Create hypothetical ethical scenarios and discuss how each of you would respond. Explore the reasons behind your decisions and how they align or differ.

Watch a movie that involves moral dilemmas. After the film, discuss the moral ambiguities presented and how they relate to your own values and experiences.

Together

Encounter with

The Self

The scariest thing is to accept yourself completely.

Carl Jung

Moments of Self-Realization

Reflect on a time when you felt a deep sense of self-actualization.
What triggered this moment and what did you learn about yourself?

Inner Conflicts

Write about an internal conflict that challenges your sense of identity. How might resolving this conflict bring you closer to your true self?

Individual reflections

Dialogue with the Self

Imagine a conversation with your "real self." What would you ask
and what do you think your real self would say in response?

Individual reflections

Create a self-portrait that captures elements of your true self,
including aspects you're still discovering. This can be done through
drawing, painting or collage.

Create a self-portrait that captures elements of your true self, including aspects you're still discovering. This can be done through drawing, painting or collage.

Letter to your True Self

Write a letter to your true self, expressing your hopes, fears and questions. Reflect on what writing this letter reveals about your journey toward self-understanding.

Letter to Your True Self

Write a letter to your true self, expressing your hopes, fears and questions. Reflect on what writing this letter reveals about your journey toward self-understanding.

Share your ideas from individual reflections with your partner. Discuss how these self-realizations impact your relationship.

Each partner describes what they believe to be their true self. Discuss how these self-perceptions align with or differ from how you view each other.

Discuss ways you can support each other to become more aligned with your true self. This could include encouraging individual hobbies, goals, or self-care practices.

Develop a vision for your future together that honors each partner's true self. Use creative means such as a vision board or written plan.

Transformation

You cannot return to consciousness without pain.

Carl Jung

Personal Transformation

Reflect on a significant change you have experienced in your life. What were the catalysts for this change and how do you think it has affected your true self?

Lessons from the Shadow

Consider a dark aspect you have faced. Write about the lessons this aspect has taught you and how it has contributed to your transformation.

Future Growth

Visualize where you see your personal growth going. What transformations do you anticipate or expect and what steps can you take to facilitate this growth?

Letter to the Past Self

Write a letter to your past self at a crucial moment of transformation. Offer support, understanding, and insight from their current perspective.

THE *Gratitude* JAR

Practice a meditation focused on gratitude for your journey, including the challenging parts. Reflect on how this gratitude shapes your vision of your personal transformation.

THE *Gratitude* JAR

Practice a meditation focused on gratitude for your journey, including the challenging parts. Reflect on how this gratitude shapes your vision of your personal transformation.

Share insights from your individual reflections. Discuss how your personal transformations have impacted your relationship.

Develop a small ritual to celebrate and recognize each person's growth and transformations. It could be a regular check-in, a special activity, or a symbolic gesture.

Take turns discussing one aspect of your transformation. The listener practices reflective listening, focusing on understanding and empathy without judgment.

Supporting Each Other's Growth

Identify ways you can support each other in your ongoing transformations. Create a plan to provide encouragement and understanding.

Together

Joint Vision

Discuss and create a joint vision for your future, considering how both transformations will shape this journey.

Conclusion

As you come to the conclusion of this guided journal, it is important to reflect on the journey you have taken, both individually and as a couple. By participating in the prompts and exercises, you have explored the depths of your unconscious, confronted repressed desires, understood the dynamics of projection, and embraced the process of integration. They have navigated the complexities of individuation, moral ambiguity, and encountered their true selves, culminating in a transformative experience that has likely reshaped both their personal identities and their relationship.

Reflections on the trip:

- Personal Growth: Reflect on how you have personally grown throughout this journey. What insights about yourself have been the most profound?
- Relationship Evolution: Consider how your relationship has evolved. How has your bond strengthened and how have you learned to better support each other?
- Challenges and Triumphs: Recognize the challenges you faced and the triumphs you achieved. Every step, whether easy or difficult, is a valuable part of your growth.

Going forward:

- Continued Exploration: Encourage each other to continue exploring and growing. This journal is a tool you can turn to whenever you need information or inspiration.
- Open Communication: Maintain the open lines of communication you have established. Regularly share your feelings, thoughts, and discoveries with each other.
- Support each other: Commit to supporting each other's ongoing journey of self-discovery and personal growth, recognizing that this process is constantly evolving.
- Embrace change: Be open to the changes that come with growth. As you both transform, so will your relationship. Embrace these changes with understanding and love.

Remember, the journey of self-discovery and relationship growth is not linear. It is a continuous and evolving process that requires patience, understanding and compassion. By participating in this work, you have taken important steps toward a deeper connection with yourselves and with others. Continue with the ideas and lessons you have learned and allow them to guide you on your continued journey toward a fulfilling and authentic life and relationship.

for getting this book and for making it all the way to the end!

Before you go, I wanted to ask you for one small favor.
Could you please consider posting a review?

Because posting a review is the best and easiest way to
support the work of independent authors like me.

Your feedback will help me a ton!

>>Leave a review on Amazon US<<

CALLIE PARKER
SHADOW
WORK
FOR COUPLES
A Guide to Strengthen Your Relationship,
Build Trust and Understanding, and
Cultivate Lasting Love

THE
SHADOW
WORK
JOURNAL AND
WORKBOOK
FOR COUPLES
CALLIE PARKER

Shadow
Work
for
Teens
A Guide for Teenagers and Young Adults
to Overcome Inner Challenges, Build
Confidence, and Practice Self-Love
CALLIE PARKER

The
Shadow
Work
Journal
for
Teens
Guided Prompts and Activities for Inner
Healing, Building Confidence, and
Practicing Self-Love
CALLIE PARKER

CALLIE PARKER
SHADOW
WORK
LGBTQ+
EDITION
A Guide to Inner
Healing and Self-Love

CALLIE PARKER
THE
SHADOW
WORK JOURNAL
LGBTQ+
EDITION

The Ultimate Self-Help Narcissistic Abuse Recovery Book

Narcissistic Abuse Recovery

Childhood Trauma and Recovery

Healing Your Inner Child (Childhood Trauma and Recovery Workbook)